Examining Issues Through
POLITICAL CARTOONS

Euthanasia

Titles in the Examining Issues Through Political Cartoons series include:

Civil Rights
The Death Penalty
Euthanasia
The Nazis
Watergate

EXAMINING ISSUES THROUGH
POLITICAL CARTOONS

Euthanasia

Edited by William Dudley

Daniel Leone, *President*
Bonnie Szumski, *Publisher*
Scott Barbour, *Managing Editor*

GREENHAVEN PRESS
SAN DIEGO, CALIFORNIA

THOMSON

GALE

Detroit • New York • San Diego • San Francisco
Boston • New Haven, Conn. • Waterville, Maine
London • Munich

Library of Congress Cataloging-in-Publication Data
Euthanasia / William Dudley, book editor.
    p. cm. — (Examining issues through political cartoons)
Includes bibliographical references and index.
    ISBN 0-7377-1103-5 (pbk. : alk. paper)
    ISBN 0-7377-1104-3 (lib. bdg. : alk. paper)
    1. Euthanasia—Moral and ethical aspects.
I. Dudley, William, 1964–   . II. Series.

Cover photo: Steiner. © Peter Steiner.
Reprinted with permission.

Copyright © 2002 by Greenhaven Press,
an imprint of The Gale Group
10911 Technology Place
San Diego, CA 92127
Printed in the U.S.A.

Contents

Foreword   6

Introduction   8

Chapter 1: Would Mercy Killing Benefit
           Patients?   18
  Preface   19

Chapter 2: Is Euthanasia Part of a "Slippery
           Slope" of Unethical Killing?   28
  Preface   29

Chapter 3: Should Doctors Be Permitted
           to Assist in Suicide?   37
  Preface   38

Chapter 4: The Supreme Court Considers
           the "Right to Die"   50
  Preface   51

Organizations to Contact   59

For Further Research   61

Index   63

Foreword

Political cartoons, also called editorial cartoons, are drawings that do what editorials do with words—express an opinion about a newsworthy event or person. They typically appear in the opinion pages of newspapers, sometimes in support of that day's written editorial, but more often making their own comment on the day's events. Political cartoons first gained widespread popularity in Great Britain and the United States in the 1800s when engravings and other drawings skewering political figures were fashionable in illustrated newspapers and comic magazines. By the beginning of the 1900s, editorial cartoons were an established feature of daily newspapers. Today, they can be found throughout the globe in newspapers, magazines, and online publications and the Internet.

Art Wood, both a cartoonist and a collector of cartoons, writes in his book *Great Cartoonists and Their Art*:

> Day in and day out the cartoonist mirrors history; he reduces complex facts into understandable and artistic terminology. He is a political commentator and at the same time an artist.

The distillation of ideas into images is what makes political cartoons a valuable resource for studying social and historical topics. Editorial cartoons have a point to express. Analyzing them involves determining both what the cartoon's point is and how it was made.

Sometimes, the point made by the cartoon may be one that the reader disagrees with, or considers offensive. Such cartoons expose readers to new ideas and thereby challenge them to analyze and question their own opinions and assumptions. In some extreme cases, cartoons provide vivid examples of the thoughts that lie behind heinous acts; for example, the cartoons created by the Nazis illustrate the anti-Semitism that led to the mass persecution of Jews.

Examining controversial ideas is but one way the study of political cartoons can enhance and develop critical thinking skills. Another aspect to cartoons is that they can use symbols to make their point quickly. For example, in a cartoon in *Euthanasia*, Chuck Asay depicts supporters of a legal "right to die" by assisted suicide as vultures. Vultures are birds that eat dead and dying animals and are often a symbol of repulsive and cowardly predators who take advantage of those who have met misfortune or are vulnerable. The reader can infer that Asay is expressing his opposition to physician-assisted suicide by suggesting that its supporters are just as loathsome as vultures. Asay thus makes his point through a quick symbolic association.

An important part of critical thinking is examining ideas and arguments in their historical context. Political cartoonists (reasonably) assume that the typical reader of a newspaper's editorial page already has a basic knowledge of current issues and newsworthy people. Understanding and appreciating political cartoons often requires such knowledge, as well as a familiarity with common icons and symbolic figures (such as Uncle Sam's representing the United States). The need for contextual information becomes especially apparent in historical cartoons. For example, although most people know who Adolf Hitler is, a lack of familiarity with other German political figures of the 1930s may create difficulty in fully understanding cartoons about Nazi Germany made in that era.

Providing such contextual information is one important way that Greenhaven's Examining Issues Through Political Cartoons series seeks to make this unique and revealing resource conveniently accessible to students. Each volume presents a representative and diverse collection of political cartoons focusing on a particular current or historical topic. An introductory essay provides a general overview of the subject matter. Each cartoon is then presented with accompanying information including facts about the cartoonist and information and commentary on the cartoon itself. Finally, each volume contains additional informational resources, including listings of books, articles, and websites; an index; and (for historical topics) a chronology of events. Taken together, the contents of each anthology constitute an amusing and informative resource for students of historical and social topics.

Introduction

The word *euthanasia* comes from two Greek words: *eu* (good) and *thanatos* (death). The English scholar and statesman Sir Francis Bacon coined the term in the early seventeenth century. Bacon argued that physicians, in addition to preserving health, curing disease, and prolonging life, ought to have the responsibility "to acquire the skill and bestow the attention whereby the dying may pass more easily and quietly out of life" in cases in which cure and relief of suffering are not possible.

Nearly four centuries later, in contemporary America, many people have argued that doctors today fail in that task. Advances in medical science have enabled physicians to cure many previously fatal diseases and to postpone death, but they have also in many instances prolonged the process of dying. Terminally ill people often find themselves confined in impersonal hospital environments, cut off from friends and family. In many cases, they may suffer from severe pain and the loss of independence and a sense of dignity. Some people have argued that the best course in such cases is the merciful ending of life—euthanasia.

Such "mercy killing" has long been the subject of controversy because it pits several ethical values in conflict with one another. These values include the preservation of life, individual autonomy, the relief of suffering, and the protection of vulnerable individuals from coercion. The issue of euthanasia thus requires people to sort through and prioritize their beliefs about fundamental values. It also involves social policy matters because a person's choices in dying are limited by laws and medical policies. As federal appeals court judge Stephen Reinhardt wrote in 1996, the issue of assisted death requires us to confront the most basic of human concerns—the mortality of self and loved ones—and to balance the interest in preserving human life against the desire to die peacefully and with dignity. . . . [This] controversy . . . may touch more people more profoundly than any other issue the courts will face in the foreseeable future.

Distinctions Between Kinds of Euthanasia

The debate over euthanasia can be confusing because the term itself can be defined and categorized in different ways. The term *euthanasia* can be defined broadly to include any action that hastens the death of a person for his or her presumed benefit. But it can also be defined less broadly as the direct killing of one person by another for reasons of mercy. Thus, the much-debated topic of physician-assisted suicide (in which a doctor prescribes medication or furnishes information a patient could use to hasten his or her own death) can be considered a form of euthanasia in its broadest sense, but not in its more narrow conception.

Ethicists who discuss euthanasia generally make distinctions between *voluntary* and *involuntary* euthanasia and *active* and *passive* euthanasia. Voluntary euthanasia is performed at the patient's request and with his or her consent. Involuntary euthanasia is the killing of a patient without such consent and possibly against his or her wishes. Very few people now endorse involuntary euthanasia; it is, writer Andrew Solomon states in a 1995 article, "outside the dominant American dialogue." In most contemporary cases in which euthanasia is being debated, it is almost always voluntary euthanasia that is under discussion. (One exception is found in cases of comatose patients, who cannot express their wishes. Here, the distinction between voluntary and involuntary euthanasia is blurred. In these situations, courts have ruled that family members have the right to act on the patient's behalf, ideally in accordance with wishes made in living wills or advance directives, maintaining the principle that euthanasia must be voluntary to be permissible.)

In addition to the distinction between voluntary and involuntary euthanasia, many ethicists differentiate between active and passive euthanasia. Passive euthanasia involves withholding or removing medical treatment, such as antibiotics, kidney dialysis, or respirators, that would otherwise prolong life. Although some people remain opposed to passive euthanasia and contend that life should be preserved at all costs, the practice has been recognized as a legal right of patients who want it. Active euthanasia, on the other hand, involves a doctor or another person deliberately acting to end a patient's life—for example, by giving the person an injection of a lethal agent. Unlike passive euthanasia, active euthanasia is illegal in the United States. Physician-assisted suicide, which has both active and passive elements (for example, a doctor prescribes sleeping pills to a patient, then stands aside if the patient chooses to commit suicide by overdose), is illegal in all states except Oregon.

Ancient and Modern Debates

Today's euthanasia debate has been influenced by both classic debates on the value of human life and modern medical developments. Some ancient societies, including the ancient Greeks and Romans, recognized and in some cases practiced involuntary infant euthanasia for children with birth defects and planned suicide for the elderly. However, not everyone in those societies endorsed such practices. The Greek philosopher Hippocrates, for example, devised an oath for physicians that included the pledge "To please no one will I prescribe a deadly drug, nor give advice which may cause his death." Many doctors today still take a version of the Hippocratic oath when they enter the profession.

With the growth of Christianity and its influence on Western civilization, euthanasia and suicide became socially proscribed and ethically abhorrent practices. Christian leaders taught that life was a gift from God and that any form of suicide was a wrongful rejection of this gift. These religious beliefs were questioned during the Enlightenment of the eighteenth century, a time when many thinkers began to cast doubt on traditional church teachings as being irrational and oppressive. Some, such as the French philosopher Voltaire, argued that suicide was a matter of personal choice and a rational option in some circumstances.

This divide between religious and secular thinking remains today. The Roman Catholic Church, for example, continues to oppose active euthanasia and assisted suicide, arguing in a 1995 papal encyclical that "euthanasia is a grave violation of the law of God." Most branches of Christianity, Judaism, and Islam oppose active euthanasia. Euthanasia advocates often accuse their opponents of imposing their religious beliefs on others. However, religion is not the sole determinant of people's positions on euthanasia. Some Christians and other religious believers support euthanasia, and many nonbelievers oppose euthanasia without invoking religious reasons.

Medical Developments and the Modern Euthanasia Debate

The ethical dilemmas of euthanasia became more relevant during the twentieth century, largely because of advances in medicine. Prior to the twentieth century, most deaths were fast ones caused by infectious diseases that doctors could do little to stop. However, over the course of the century, the combination of better living conditions and the use of antibiotics brought many infectious diseases under control, at least in developed nations. Growing numbers of people survived into old age (the average life expectancy for Americans jumped from forty-seven in 1900 to seventy-one in 1970). Instead of pneumonia or some other disease that killed rapidly, people were more likely to get cancer, heart disease, or another debilitating condition that often meant a painful, lingering death and a slow loss of physical and mental abilities.

In the 1930s, several organizations in the United States and Great Britain were founded to promote the idea of voluntary euthanasia. At first, these organizations remained very small and had little influence. But a court case in the 1970s brought publicity and new momentum to their cause.

Karen Ann Quinlan's Tragedy

On April 14, 1975, a twenty-one-year-old New Jersey woman named Karen Ann Quinlan went to a party. There, after ingesting a mixture of drugs and alcohol, she lapsed into unconsciousness and stopped breathing. She was rushed to a hospital, where she was connected to a respirator, a device that forces air in and out of the lungs of people who have stopped breathing. The machine kept Karen Ann Quinlan alive, but she never again regained consciousness. She was in what was termed a persistent vegetative state.

Over the next several months, Karen's parents watched as she lost weight and her contracting muscles drew her into a twisted position. They were told that her brain was probably damaged beyond repair and that she would never regain full consciousness. At the end

11

of July 1975, the parents determined that only the respirator was keeping their daughter from an unavoidable natural death, so they asked the hospital to turn it off. The hospital refused, saying that doing so was against the principle of medical ethics that prohibited them from taking any action that could cause or hasten death.

The Quinlans sued for the legal right to turn off the respirator. The state judge who heard the case turned down their request to cease medical treatment. He argued that although Karen had the right to refuse life-sustaining treatment, her inability to communicate such wishes meant that the government must take on the duty to preserve life. However, on appeal, the New Jersey State Supreme Court ruled in the parents' favor, arguing that parents or guardians could make such a decision in order to let a person "die with dignity." The decision touched off a controversy because it directly challenged the view that life should be preserved at all costs. (Ironically, after the respirator was removed, Quinlan lived and breathed on her own until 1985 without ever regaining consciousness.)

The Quinlan case had a significant impact on the issue of how medicine should treat patients. It publicized the right of patients to create advance directives or living wills, documents that spell out what treatments they are to receive if ill or injured. Prior to that, few patients bothered to put their wishes about accepting or refusing medical treatment in writing, and when such documents did exist, hospitals frequently ignored them. In the wake of the Quinlan case, more patients filled out advance directive forms. Perhaps more important, such directives were given legal standing and force by state and federal laws, and doctors were protected from being sued for failing to treat terminal illnesses.

In 1990, in the case of *Cruzan v. Director, Missouri Dept. of Health*, another instance in which parents wished to end treatment of a comatose daughter, the U.S. Supreme Court endorsed passive euthanasia. The Court ruled that incurably ill patients had the legal right to refuse life-sustaining treatment, including the provision of food and water. The Supreme Court's endorsement of passive, voluntary euthanasia is shared by medical associations, many religious groups, and (according to polls) about three-fourths of the American public.

In Canada, a somewhat similar court case also paved the way for acceptance of passive euthanasia. A young woman with a rare paralytic disease (Guillain-Barré syndrome) wished to have her artificial breathing mechanism disconnected, but was refused on the grounds that such a request would kill her. A Quebec superior court judge authorized the woman's physician to remove the respirator.

More Active Aid in Dying Sought

For some people, however, the right to be allowed to die through passive means was not enough. They argued that terminally ill and suffering people should have not only the right to refuse treatment but the legal right for active assistance in ending their lives. Such a "right to die" should be considered part of the freedoms guaranteed to Americans by the U.S. Constitution, they asserted. A way to guarantee that right, many argued, was physician-assisted suicide.

The issue of physician-assisted suicide gained national prominence in 1991 through the publication of an article and a book. The article, in the *New England Journal of Medicine*, was written by a doctor named Timothy E. Quill. He described a case in which a longtime patient who suffered from acute leukemia asked him for the means to end her life should she find it intolerable. After unsuccessfully attempting to dissuade her, Quill prescribed her sleeping pills and told her how many pills were needed to help her sleep—and how many would be necessary to commit suicide. The patient killed herself four months later. Quill's article brought out into the open the experiences other doctors shared but did not proclaim—that of quietly helping patients to die.

That same year, the book *Final Exit: The Practice of Self-Deliverance and Assisted Suicide for the Dying* was a surprise success. Primarily a guide to potentially lethal drugs and their effects, the volume sold over half a million copies. Its author, Derek Humphry, was the founder of the Hemlock Society, a right-to-die group; in 1975 he killed his first wife at her request as she suffered from terminal cancer, an experience he had described in a previous book. *Final Exit's* popularity was seen as indicative of how important the issue of dying was to the American public.

Part of the subsequent public debate over physician-assisted suicide was regarding whether patients had sufficient choices in end-of-life care. Opponents of assisted suicide argued that the care of the dying had improved much since the Karen Ann Quinlan case. Doctors were receiving more training in palliative care, tending to the patient's comfort and quality of life rather than treating the disease. Hospices—institutions designed to provide for the physical and emotional needs of dying people—were becoming an increasingly popular option. In addition, more doctors gave their dying and suffering patients large amounts of narcotics such as morphine, justifying their actions on the principle of "double effect"—that is, if the primary purpose of the medication was to relieve suffering, it was permitted even if it shortened life. Whether these options are sufficient for dying patients is in dispute. "I submit that the answer to the problem of assisted suicide lies not in more euthanasia but in more hospice care," writes psychologist and author M. Scott Peck, suggesting that if adequate hospice care was provided for all patients, there would be no need for euthanasia or assisted suicide. However, Quill, Humphry, and others contend that such alternatives still fall short of what dying patients need. "Dressing up hospice care as a panacea," writes John L. Miller in the *American Journal of Hospice and Palliative Care*, "and as the only moral alternative to physician-assisted suicide, is unhelpful and inadequate."

Legal Challenges

Both Humphry and Quill were involved in legal challenges to state laws against assisted suicide (in most states, suicide was not a crime but helping someone else commit suicide was). The movement to establish a constitutionally protected "right to die" and to legalize physician-assisted suicide experienced both accomplishments and setbacks during the 1990s. Advocates of legalizing physician-assisted suicide succeeded in placing measures on the agenda of state legislatures and on ballots for voter approval in several states, but in most cases the laws failed to attain a majority of votes.

Right-to-die activists then tried a different tactic, filing lawsuits in Washington and New York that claimed that the states' bans on assisted suicide violated the constitutional rights of terminal patients. In 1996, federal courts in New York and Washington ruled that the state laws were unconstitutional—that assistance in dying was indeed a constitutional right. The U.S. Supreme Court, however, overturned these decisions in 1997, arguing that the Constitution does not guarantee individuals the right to assisted suicide or to euthanasia. However, it left the door open for states to decide whether to ban or legalize assisted suicide.

The Supreme Court's ruling, therefore, meant that physician-assisted suicide would remain legal in Oregon, where voters had passed the Death with Dignity Act into law in 1994 and reaffirmed their choice in 1997. Under its provisions, a person can obtain a lethal substance from a doctor if certain safeguards are upheld:

- The request must come from an adult resident of Oregon who is mentally competent and terminally ill.

- Two physicians must examine the patient to confirm the terminal diagnosis and to confirm the patient's mental competency to make decisions; they can call for a mental health evaluation if necessary.

- Patients must wait fifteen days between a doctor's visit and the writing of a prescription, plus an additional two days for the prescription for the death-causing medication to be filled.

- Prescriptions must be reported to the state health department.

Between 1997 and 2001, seventy Oregon residents used the law to end their lives. In November 2001, Attorney General John Ashcroft announced that doctors who prescribed federally controlled substances for the purpose of assisted suicide would have their drug-prescription licenses revoked, an announcement that reversed previous federal policy and placed the legal status of physician-assisted suicide in Oregon in jeopardy.

Economic Pressures and the "Duty" to Die

Many who oppose physician-assisted suicide argue that, although a "right to die" might sound attractive to Americans who value their civil rights, such a right could evolve into a more ominous "duty to die." Many express concern that if euthanasia or physician-assisted suicide became a standard and recognized practice rather than something forbidden by law or medical ethics, people might feel pressured or coerced to exercise this "right" for reasons not related to ending physical suffering or terminal illness. Yale Kamisur, a University of Michigan law professor, raised such questions in a 1969 article. If voluntary active euthanasia were legal, he asked,

> Will we not sweep up, in the process, some who are not really tired of life, but think others are tired of them; some who

do not really want to die, but who feel they should not live on, because to do so when there looms the legal alternative of euthanasia is to do a selfish or cowardly act? Will not some feel an obligation to have themselves "eliminated" in order that funds allocated for their terminal care might be better used by their families or, financial worries aside, in order to relieve their families of the emotional strain involved?

In examining the question of whether euthanasia would turn into a "duty" to die, the economic realities of America's health care system must be taken into account. Runaway health costs are a major concern for individuals, their families, and American society as a whole. A large proportion of health care expenses stem from the care of chronic diseases among the elderly. In response to spiraling costs, medical insurers in the 1980s and 1990s turned to health maintenance organizations (HMOs) and other forms of managed care, which sought to control costs by limiting what was deemed unnecessary and expensive care. Similar measures were taken in government-run systems such as Great Britain's National Health Service. Managed care techniques cut rising costs by eliminating waste and unnecessary treatment, but critics often argued that they denied essential services to people in need.

Given the fact that a single lethal dose of medication costs considerably less than months or years of hospitalization or high-tech care, opponents of assisted suicide and euthanasia often wonder if patients might be encouraged or even coerced to end their lives in order to save money. "We're talking about cutting Medicare [the U.S. government program that pays for the elderly's health care] and our social obligation to take care of the disabled, and at the same time we're also talking about physician-assisted suicide, and no one's noticing that they might come together in a very different way," warns Joanne Lynn, a specialist in the care of the elderly. Lynn and other opponents of assisted suicide fear that the elderly and disabled might be tempted to take their own lives because they may be denied nursing and home care that could maintain their comfort and independence. Those who fear that cost containment could become a rationale for voluntary (or even involuntary) euthanasia cite the writings of some euthanasia advocates. Derek Humphry, author of *Final Exit*, cites costs as one reason for planned suicide in his 1998 book (with coauthor Mary Clement), *Freedom to Die: People, Politics, and the Right-to-Die Movement:*

> A new study of seriously ill people in hospitals found that 30 percent of those surveyed said they would rather *die* than live permanently in a nursing home. . . .Why do we, as a nation, not allow these people to die. . . ? Their lives would conclude with dignity and self-respect, and one measure of cost containment would be in place.

However, others do not believe that legalizing assisted suicide or voluntary euthanasia would inevitably lead to coerced or involuntary euthanasia. They argue that similar arguments were made during Karen Ann Quinlan's case, but society's subsequent acceptance of passive euthanasia and living wills showed that such forecasts of impending forced euthanasia were unfounded. Safeguards, such as those in the Oregon law, and rules limiting euthanasia and assisted suicide to the terminally ill are an adequate answer to the objection of possible coercion of the elderly and sick. "It seems impossible that involuntary active euthanasia would ever be a problem in a liberal society such as the United States," writes medical school director Chris Hackler. "If ever there were a strongly held moral consensus, it is that killing innocent people against their wishes is wrong."

A Continuing National Debate

Even assuming that the moral consensus described by Hackler continues, America remains divided on death and dying issues. While society has reached a rough moral consensus on the acceptability of voluntary passive euthanasia (something that did not exist in 1970), no such consensus exists on assisted suicide and direct mercy killing. As long as people must face chronic, debilitating illness and a prolonged dying process for themselves and their loved ones, this lack of consensus means that for many Americans, defining and attaining a "good death" will continue to remain a troubling moral dilemma.

Chapter 1

Would Mercy Killing Benefit Patients?

Preface

The cartoons in this chapter all involve variations on the same basic scenario—a scenario that lies at the heart of the euthanasia debate. A person lies in a bed suffering from an illness. Doctors may be able to keep the patient alive, but cannot offer a cure for him. Questions are raised: At what point is death more merciful and humane than continued treatment? And if there is such a point, should doctors and others take steps to hasten that outcome? Is "mercy killing" a contradiction in terms?

Variations on this scenario might alter how people answer the above questions. Many people make a distinction between whether an illness is terminal or not, arguing that assisted suicide or euthanasia may be acceptable in the former circumstance but not in the latter. Others distinguish between conscious patients, who are able to express their own wishes, and comatose patients, whose decisions must be made for them by doctors or relatives. Many people believe that a hastened death is more acceptable if the patient is unable to breathe or eat independently and must rely on ventilators or artificial feeding tubes; people draw a moral distinction between "pulling the plug" on artificial life support (acceptable) and actively killing an ill patient who is not on life support (not acceptable). The cartoonists featured in this chapter provide differing perspectives on whether acting to hasten a patient's death is truly an act of mercy and in the patient's best interests.

Examining Cartoon 1:
"What? And Play God?"

About the Cartoon

In this cartoon by Tom Toles, a patient asks a doctor to let him die. The doctor objects, saying that to do so would be tantamount to playing God. However, the patient is already being kept alive by numerous artificial means, suggesting that the doctor is essentially *already* playing God by refusing to let death take its "natural" course. The cartoon criticizes the medical profession as being overly enamored of technology and insensitive to the suffering caused by the commitment to extend life by any means possible.

The euthanasia the cartoon is referring to is both voluntary (the patient is asking for it) and passive (it involves withholding of artificial life-support systems), as opposed to "active" euthanasia in which the doctor would perform a lethal injection or otherwise actively cause the patient to die.

Toles's cartoons often feature an extra comment in the bottom corner (next to a self-portrait of the cartoonist). This cartoon's extra punch line refers to the "Sweet Chariot" of death that is the subject of the famous American spiritual "Swing Low, Sweet Chariot."

About the Cartoonist

Tom Toles is the political cartoonist for the *Buffalo News* and winner of the 1990 Pulitzer Prize for editorial cartooning.

Examining Cartoon 2:
"3 out of 4 Favor Euthanasia"

About the Cartoon

Like the preceding cartoon by Tom Toles, this cartoon by Wayne Stayskal features an elderly patient who is apparently hospitalized and dependent on machines for life support. However, the attitude of the patient is quite different. Whereas Toles's patient had asked his doctor to let him die, Stayskal's patient, after reading a newspaper headline stating that "3 out of 4 Favor Euthanasia," has barricaded his door with a chair. *He* does not want to be euthanized and is now afraid that others might attempt to do the "merciful" thing and kill him.

About the Cartoonist

Wayne Stayskal is the editorial cartoonist for the *Tampa Tribune*. His work has been collected in several books including *Liberals for Lunch*.

Examining Cartoon 3:
"It Would Be Cruel to Prolong the Inevitable."

It WOULD Be CRUEL to PROLONG the iNeVitaBLe.

It'S iNeVitaBLe to PROLONG the cRUeLty.

About the Cartoon

Pets, unlike people, are routinely euthanized when they are sick or unwanted. This two-panel cartoon by Kirk Anderson accentuates the differences between how dying pets and people are treated. It depicts a family and doctor confronting two situations involving a sick and presumably dying patient. They have identical poses and expressions. In one case, they apparently have decided to euthanize their pet dog. In the other panel, they have no choice—their elderly relative is fated to be kept alive by machinery regardless of whether she suffers or not. Anderson's captions suggest that he believes the dog may be better off than the person.

About the Cartoonist

Since 1995 Kirk Anderson has been the editorial cartoonist for the *St. Paul Pioneer Press*. His work has been featured in numerous newspapers, magazines, and websites.

Examining Cartoon 4:

"... As Soon as I Get Permission from Her Owner!"

About the Cartoon

This cartoon by Chuck Asay, like the preceding Kirk Anderson cartoon, deals with the different way in which society treats dying people and dying animals. In this cartoon, a person argues that pets can be put out of their misery and asks the doctor why he could not do the same thing for a sick patient. The doctor replies that he would have to get permission for euthanasia from the patient's owner. His answer carries the implication that neither he nor the complaining person has the right to make such a decision. The fact that Asay lets the doctor have the final word indicates his own opposition to euthanasia for humans.

About the Cartoonist

Chuck Asay is the editorial cartoonist for the *Colorado Springs Gazette-Telegraph*. His work frequently deals with religious and ethical issues.

Chapter 2

Is Euthanasia Part of a "Slippery Slope" of Unethical Killing?

EXAMINING ISSUES THROUGH
POLITICAL CARTOONS

Preface

The debate over euthanasia often centers around the so-called slippery slope argument. This argument holds that permitting one behavior will inevitably lead to a series of increasingly worse behaviors or outcomes. Opponents of euthanasia argue that if it is legalized in some circumstances, it will eventually be applied to other situations as well.

In recent years, for example, slippery slope arguments have been prominent in the debate over physician-assisted suicide (permitting doctors to assist patients to kill themselves). Proponents of doctor-assisted suicide argue that such an option should be available for people who are terminally ill and who wish to control the circumstances of their death. Critics argue that if voluntary assisted suicide were legalized, the social acceptance of euthanasia for people who are mentally incompetent, depressed, handicapped, or simply uninsured would follow. They project a future in which people would be involuntarily euthanized to spare their families and society the economic burden of caring for them, rather than to relieve the suffering of individuals. Some have argued that this progression has already happened in Holland, the only country to legalize physician-assisted suicide. "In theory, the hastened death of Dutch patients is supposed to be a rare event, only to be used in the most intractable cases," writes euthanasia opponent Wesley J. Smith. However, he continues,

> In actual practice, . . . death-causing "medical" practices have expanded almost geometrically, demonstrating empirically the severe incline of the slippery slope. Thus, today, you need not be terminally ill to be killed by your doctor. . . .

Despite the guidelines proscribing euthanasia unless specifically requested by the patient, Dutch doctors also engage in involuntary euthanasia.

Whether such developments are in fact the inevitable outcome of legalizing physician-assisted suicide has been a hotly contested point. "We have no reason to believe that granting the terminally ill the right to voluntary, assisted suicide would somehow lead to coerced deaths," argues Barbara Dority. Proponents of physician-assisted suicide also argue that if such slippery slope scenarios exist, safeguards built into legal controls of physician-assisted suicide can prevent them from occurring.

The risk that physician-assisted suicide could lead to involuntary euthanasia is not the only example of slippery slope arguments in the euthanasia debate. Some opponents have placed euthanasia in the middle of a slippery slope that began when the United States legalized abortion in 1973. "Pro-life" abortion foes sometimes argue that legalized abortion encourages a social ethic that justifies killing human lives because they are inconvenient and burdensome for others. Such arguments could also be made to justify ending the lives of the elderly or handicapped for similar reasons. Thus, in this view, legalized abortion has started America on a slippery slope of killing for convenience that could lead to voluntary, and later, involuntary euthanasia. As in the assisted suicide debate, many have attacked such slippery slope arguments as fallacious, asserting that there is no logical reason to assume that legalized abortion would inexorably lead to widespread euthanasia. The cartoons in this chapter explore various facets of the slippery slope argument against euthanasia, including connections between euthanasia and abortion.

Examining Cartoon 1:
"Sorry, Gramps."

About the Cartoon

Euthanasia, which remains illegal in the United States, is sometimes compared with the legal practice of abortion. Many people who oppose abortion suggest that the rationales behind terminating unwanted pregnancies could just as easily be used to justify terminating the lives of unwanted elderly people. In this view, euthanasia is a step or two down the "slippery slope" that legalized abortion creates. In the above cartoon, a woman makes arguments that are often heard in justifying abortion. However, in the final panel it is revealed that what she really wanted was not to abort her fetus, but to shoot her grandfather—an extreme form of euthanasia.

About the Cartoonist

Chip Bok is the editorial cartoonist for the *Akron Beacon Journal* and a regular contributing cartoonist for *Reason* magazine. His awards include the 1995 National Catoonist Society award for best editorial cartoonist.

Examining Cartoon 2:
"I'm Sorry . . ."

About the Cartoon

This cartoon, like the previous one, makes a connection between euthanasia and abortion, but with a somewhat different emphasis. In the cartoon, a doctor solemnly informs the spouse of a man whose medical status is "vegetable" that he cannot "pull the plug" on the patient's life support because "mercy killing is against the law." Across the hall is a place where abortions, which are legal, are performed. The cartoon can be interpreted as an attack on the hypocrisy of a society that forbids any killing that would prevent pointless suffering while allowing the deaths that result from legalized abortion.

About the Cartoonist

Ed Gamble joined the *Florida Times-Union* in Jacksonville as its first staff political cartoonist in 1980. His honors include two Florida Press Association awards. His work has been collected in the book *You Get Two for the Price of One.*

Examining Cartoon 3:

"I Hope the Supreme Court..."

About the Cartoon

A concern many people have about legalizing euthanasia or doctor-assisted suicide is that people may be killed not to relieve pain and suffering, but rather to save money that would otherwise be spent keeping them alive. Mike Smith raises this possibility in the above cartoon that also pokes fun at HMOs (health maintenance organizations). Critics of HMOs often accuse them of refusing to pay for needed medical treatments and for emphasizing profits over the health of their enrollees. In this instance, an HMO official expresses to a patient his hope that the Supreme Court would approve physician-assisted suicide. The obvious implication is that HMOs find such a development desirable because it would save them money.

About the Cartoonist

Mike Smith is the editorial cartoonist for the *Las Vegas Sun*.

Chapter 3

Should Doctors Be Permitted to Assist in Suicide?

EXAMINING ISSUES THROUGH
POLITICAL CARTOONS

Preface

Passive euthanasia is the withholding or withdrawing of life-sustaining treatment from people who are terminally ill and nearing death. This practice has been officially accepted by the American Medical Association (AMA) in cases where terminally ill individuals or their legal surrogates request it to relieve suffering. Active euthanasia—the deliberate administration of a lethal agent to a patient—has been rejected by the AMA as "fundamentally incompatible with the physician's role as healer" and a source of "serious societal risks." It remains illegal in the United States. (In 2001, Holland legalized active euthanasia in some circumstances.)

A controversial option that lies somewhere between active and passive euthanasia is physician-assisted suicide. In this alternative, the physician does not administer the lethal agent, but provides the patient information and the means to commit suicide. In recent years most of the public debate and controversy over euthanasia-related issues has focused on this practice.

While many people advocate physician-assisted suicide as a means to ease the suffering of dying patients, others believe the practice goes against fundamental medical ethics. The Hippocratic oath, a pledge doctors take that dates back to ancient times, includes the following:

> To please no one will I prescribe a deadly drug, nor give advice which may cause his death.

The AMA has opposed physician-assisted suicide for the same reasons it opposes active euthanasia.

During the 1990s several states debated whether to legalize doctor-assisted suicide. (In most states, suicide is legal, but assisting someone else's suicide is not.) Right-to-die organizations were able to place initiatives on the ballots of several states for voters to decide. In some states, including Michigan and California, laws legalizing physician-assisted suicide were rejected. In one state—Oregon— voters in 1994 passed a measure that legalized physician-assisted suicide for mentally competent, terminally ill residents who requested it. This law survived a court challenge and was again upheld by voters in 1997. In 1998, its first year of operation, twenty-three patients received prescriptions for lethal drugs, of which fifteen used them to kill themselves. In November 2001, however, Attorney General John Ashcroft placed an obstacle to assisted suicide in Oregon by barring use of federally controlled substances for such a purpose (Ashcroft's ruling was temporarily blocked by the courts, leaving Oregon's assisted suicide program in legal limbo).

While physician-assisted suicide was being debated in medical journals and newspaper editorial pages, the most visible spokesperson for physician-assisted suicide—the person whom many identified with the movement—was Jack Kevorkian. From 1990 to 1998, he claimed to have assisted in the suicide of more than one hundred persons, usually in defiance of state and local laws. Critics of Kevorkian —which included both proponents and opponents of legalizing physician-assisted suicide—questioned his motives and methods. Kevorkian courted media attention and rarely knew the people he assisted, many of whom were not terminally ill. Furthermore, his ideas often verged on the bizarre (among his proposed practices were medical experiments on death-row inmates). Kevorkian's medical license was revoked, and he was tried five times in Michigan for murder or assisted suicide. The first four trials resulted in acquittals or mistrials. A fifth trial in 1999, involving a case in which he administered the lethal drugs to a patient himself, resulted in a murder conviction and a lengthy prison sentence. His imprisonment took away a favorite target of editorial cartoonists, but did not stop the underlying debates over physician-assisted suicide.

Examining Cartoon 1:
"A Disposable Society"

MICHAEL RAMIREZ

SUPPORT DOCTOR-ASSISTED SUICIDE

HIPPOCRATIC OATH

OREGON

A DISPOSABLE SOCIETY

About the Cartoon

In 1994 Oregon voters passed an initiative that legalized physician-aided suicide. They reaffirmed their choice in November 1997, when they defeated a measure that would have repealed the 1994 law. As of 2001, Oregon remains the only U.S. state in which doctor-assisted suicide is legal. The above cartoon was created shortly after the 1997 vote. Cartoonist Michael Ramirez depicts a pile of trash that includes a discarded human body in a garbage can and a piece of paper labeled "HIPPOCRATIC OATH." Several arguments frequently made by opponents of physician-assisted suicide are alluded to here. One is that physician-assisted suicide devalues the inherent worth of human life and that it places humans on par with other objects in America's "disposable society" that can be discarded when they are obsolete or no longer valued. In addition, physician-assisted suicide "trashes" the Hippocratic oath—the two-thousand-year-old promise that most doctors take, the classic version of which includes the pledge: "To please no one will I prescribe a deadly drug, nor give advice which may cause his death." Critics argue that allowing physicians to assist in suicide jeopardizes the doctor-patient relationship because the patient loses trust that the doctor is acting in the patient's interests.

About the Cartoonist

Michael Ramirez won the Pulitzer Prize for editorial cartooning in 1994 when he worked for the *Memphis Commercial Appeal.* He is now on the staff of the *Los Angeles Times;* his syndicated work also appears in *USA Today.*

Examining Cartoon 2:
"You Have Been Found Guilty..."

About the Cartoon

In 1994 Oregon became the first state to pass a law legalizing physician-assisted suicide. Opponents of doctor-assisted suicide in the U.S. Congress subsequently proposed and debated (but failed to pass) measures that would prohibit using federally controlled substances such as barbiturates and painkillers for the purpose of euthanasia or suicide.

This cartoon by Don Wright is critical of these proposed measures. It portrays Congress as an overbearing judge passing sentence on a doctor who has committed what many would consider to be a morally defensible action. To give the cartoon an ironic twist, the cartoonist has the "judge" proclaim that life is a precious gift, then sentence the defendant to death. The legislation that inspired the cartoon did provide for stiff sentences of up to twenty years imprisonment for doctors who violated it, but not capital punishment. The drawing is an example of how cartoonists use exaggeration to make a point.

About the Cartoonist

Don Wright gave up a photography career to become the political cartoonist for the *Miami News* in 1963. He won Pulitzer Prizes for editorial cartooning in 1966 and 1980. In 1989 he moved to the *West Palm Beach Post*. His work has been collected in several books including *Wright On!* and *Wright Side Up*.

Examining Cartoon 3:
"Just Call Me God!"

About the Cartoon

On December 4, 1995, Physicians for Mercy, a group of doctors and medical specialists in Michigan, held a press conference in which they presented guidelines on how doctors could help patients who requested suicide. (Michigan had been the site of several widely publicized criminal trials involving assisted suicide.) The above cartoon is a response to Physicians for Mercy and their endorsement of doctor-assisted suicide. The doctor in the cartoon casually tells the patient to "just call me God." Critics of physician-assisted suicide often argue that doctors are acting beyond their moral authority—in essence playing God—when they act to end a person's life.

About the Cartoonist

Wayne Stayskal is the editorial cartoonist for the *Tampa Tribune*. His work has been collected in several books including *Liberals for Lunch*.

Examining Cartoon 4:
"The Suicide of Adam"

The Suicide of Adam

About the Cartoon

In the 1990s Jack Kevorkian, a pathologist and author, was one of the leading public advocates of euthanasia and assisted suicide. In June 1990 he provided a machine of his invention to Janice Adkins, who used it to kill herself. Kevorkian's outspoken views and his involvement in assisting many ill patients like Adkins to commit suicide made him a frequent target of editorial cartoonists. This cartoon, first published in 1990, is a critical picture of Kevorkian that is rich with cultural references. Titled "The Suicide of Adam," the cartoon is a parody of the *Creation of Adam*, a famous religious painting by the Italian renaissance artist Michelangelo. Michelangelo's original painting depicted a reclining Adam receiving life from an outstretched finger of God, who was drawn as a benevolent and powerful humanlike figure accompanied by angels (according to the Bible, Adam was the first human that God created). In this parody, Adam instead receives a lethal injection from a not-so-benevolent-looking Kevorkian and his "suicide machine." Kevorkian, the cartoonist suggests, is putting himself in place of God, but as a bringer of death rather than life. Instead of angels, he is accompanied by monsters, including the Frankenstein creature, itself a reference to novelist Mary Shelley's fictional scientist who attempted to play God by creating artificial human life with dire results.

About the Cartoonist

Steve Benson, a longtime staff cartoonist for the *Arizona Republic*, won a Pulitzer Prize for his work in 1993.

Examining Cartoon 5:
"Dr. Kevorkian, How Long Did It Take You . . ."

About the Cartoon

Jack Kevorkian became known as "Doctor Death" during the 1990s for his efforts to help ill and suffering patients commit suicide. By his own admission, he helped 130 people kill themselves using devices of his invention. He was tried four times on criminal charges by the state of Michigan; the trials resulted in three acquittals and one mistrial.

In 1998, shortly after a new Michigan law making assisted suicide a felony took effect, he made a videotape of the death of Thomas

Youk, a person suffering from Lou Gehrig's disease. It was submitted to the television news program *60 Minutes* and broadcast on November 23, 1998. In the tape, Kevorkian not only helped Youk set up his suicide device, but also activated the machine itself. In doing so, he crossed what many people viewed as an important ethical line between assisted suicide and euthanasia. He was subsequently tried and convicted of second-degree murder and sent to prison.

Kevorkian's controversial actions and views, coupled with his national media exposure, led many supporters of doctor-assisted suicide to wonder whether he was helping or discrediting their cause. This cartoon, originally published right after his actions were broadcast to the nation on *60 Minutes*, implies the latter. Kevorkian is lampooned as a figure of death (with the traditional robe and scythe). His answer to reporter's question refers to his infamous television show appearance, which many believe brought the idea of assisted suicide into disrepute.

About the Cartoonist

Mike Thompson is the editorial cartoonist for the *Detroit Free Press*. His work is nationally syndicated.

Chapter 4

The Supreme Court Considers the "Right to Die"

Preface

O ver the past quarter century, the nation's courts have issued more than two hundred rulings concerning end-of-life issues; several cases reached the Supreme Court. Most of these rulings involved an individual's right to refuse medical treatment. State and federal judges have generally upheld the right of a competent adult to decide to refuse life-sustaining treatment, even if such a decision shortened the person's life. This right is believed to be rooted in common law of American and British legal tradition. "No right is held more sacred, or is more carefully guarded, by the common law, than the right of every individual to the possession and control of his own person [body]," stated the U.S. Supreme Court in 1891. This right was affirmed by the Supreme Court in *Cruzan v. Missouri Department of Health* in 1990, in which the justices ruled that the right of individuals to refuse intravenous feeding tubes was protected by the Constitution.

In recent years, the focus has shifted from the right to refuse treatment to the right to ask for a doctor's active help in dying. Right-to-die advocates argue that terminally ill people who are not dependent on life-sustaining treatment such as respirators or feeding tubes should have the legal right to ask for assistance in determining their own death. They contend that implicit in the right to refuse medical treatment that may result in one's own death is the right to seek active assistance in suicide for patients whose death requires more than "pulling the plug" on a respirator, for example. Lawsuits were filed in Washington and New York in 1994 challenging state laws against assisted suicide. In 1996, two federal appeals court panels ruled that such laws were unconstitutional —in other words, that individuals had a constitutional right to physician-assisted suicide. The cases were appealed to the Supreme Court.

In 1997, the Supreme Court unanimously reversed the lower court rulings and upheld the state laws against assisted suicide, declaring that there was no general constitutional right to physician-assisted suicide. The Court held that the government's interests in protecting life and preventing abuses against vulnerable groups outweighed the suggested "right to die." Furthermore, the justices declared that significant differences existed between people who wanted to refuse medical treatment and those who wanted active assistance in dying. Treating the two groups differently did not violate the Constitution's mandate of "equal protection of the laws," according to the Court. The ruling left open the possibility that states could craft laws permitting assisted suicide. However, the decision was generally praised by opponents of physician-assisted suicide and criticized by proponents of the practice. This chapter provides samples of cartoonists' reactions to the decisions of the Supreme Court and other judges regarding assisted suicide and the "right to die."

Examining Cartoon 1:
"Embalm Nancy Cruzan"

About the Cartoon

The Supreme Court's first case concerning the "right to die" involved Nancy Cruzan, a woman who was in a car crash that left her in a persistent vegetative state. Able to breathe but unable to feed herself, she was kept alive by a feeding tube. After several years in this condition, her parents sought legal permission to stop life support, and eventually took their case to the Supreme Court. In 1990, the Court ruled in *Cruzan v. Missouri Department of Health* that people had a constitutional right to refuse life-sustaining treatment.

However, in cases involving comatose patients such as Cruzan, the justices declared that "clear and convincing evidence" must exist that the patient would not want to be kept alive under such circumstances. The parents, utilizing testimony from Cruzan's friends, eventually obtained permission from a probate court judge to remove the feeding tube in December 1990; Cruzan died a few days later.

Nancy Cruzan's case not only involved her family and the legal system, but also became a focus of activity for many abortion protesters and anti-euthanasia activists. They contended that as long as Cruzan was living and breathing, she should be kept alive. Some of them picketed her hospital carrying signs accusing Cruzan's parents of murder by starvation. In this cartoon, published shortly after Cruzan finally passed away, Tom Toles mocks these protesters by taking their arguments one step further into absurdity. He portrays protesters carrying signs calling for the embalming of Cruzan in the hope perhaps she may yet be revived. His "extra" commentary on the bottom right corner (a feature of most of Toles's cartoons) is a sarcastic remark about Cruzan's suffering, which he apparently believes was prolonged by the lengthy legal struggle.

About the Cartoonist

Tom Toles is the political cartoonist for the *Buffalo News* and winner of the 1990 Pulitzer Prize for editorial cartooning.

Examining Cartoon 2:
"Shoo!"

About the Cartoon

In 1997 the Supreme Court ruled on two "right-to-die" cases: *Quill v. Vacco* and *Washington v. Glucksberg*. The Court ruled unanimously that Washington and New York state laws prohibiting physician-assisted suicide did not violate the U.S. Constitution. A person may have a constitutional right to refuse medical treatment, the justices declared, but not a right to have a doctor assist in committing suicide (the Supreme Court left open the possibility that states may pass laws permitting physician-assisted suicide).

The above cartoon by Chuck Asay depicts the Supreme Court justices as valiant defenders of would-be victims of physician-assisted suicide. Chief Justice William Rehnquist uses the U.S. Constitution to chase away a vulture representing "The Dr. Kevorkians." Jack Kevorkian was an outspoken advocate of physician-assisted suicide who had helped dozens of patients die. In Asay's view, Kevorkian and his supporters are like vultures who prey on the sick and dying. A minicartoon in the bottom right corner suggests that this will not be the last time the Supreme Court has to protect people from advocates of physician-assisted suicide.

About the Cartoonist

Chuck Asay is the editorial cartoonist for the *Colorado Springs Gazette-Telegraph*.

Asay. © 1997, Creators Syndicate, Inc. Reprinted with permission.

Examining Cartoon 3:

"We Thought We Were *Already* Devalued!"

About the Cartoon

In 1997 the Supreme Court agreed to hear two important cases involving physician-assisted suicide, ultimately upholding the constitutionality of state laws banning the practice. The above cartoon presents a far different image of the Supreme Court than the previous cartoon by Chuck Asay. Three of the most conservative justices (from left to right, Antonin Scalia, William Rehnquist, and Clarence Thomas) are pictured. They object to assisted suicide by arguing that it devalues human life and might lead to the devaluation of the poor, disabled, and minorities. The concluding scene and punch line imply that these people are *already* not valued very much, and raises the question of whether the justices truly care about the poor and disabled or are just using them to make a rhetorical point.

About the Cartoonist

Joel Pett is the editorial cartoonist for the *Lexington World-Ledger,* and winner of the 2000 Pulitzer Prize for editorial cartoons.

Pett. © 1997, *Lexington Herald-Leader.* Reprinted with permission.

Organizations to Contact

The editors have compiled the following list of organizations concerned with the issues featured in this book. The descriptions are derived from materials provided by the organizations. All have publications or information available for interested readers. This list was compiled on the date of publication of the present volume; the information provided here may change. Be aware that many organizations take several weeks or longer to respond to inquiries, so allow as much time as possible.

Euthanasia Prevention Coalition BC
103-2609 Westview Dr., Suite 126,
North Vancouver, BC V7N 4N2
(604) 794-3772 • fax: (604) 794-3960
website: www.epc.bc.ca

The Euthanasia Prevention Coalition opposes the promotion or legalization of euthanasia and assisted suicide. The coalition's purpose is to educate the public on risks associated with the promotion of euthanasia, increase public awareness of alternative methods for the relief of suffering, and to represent the vulnerable as an advocate before the courts on issues of euthanasia and related subjects. Press releases from the coalition are available at its website.

Euthanasia Research and Guidance Organization (ERGO)
24829 Norris Ln., Junction City, OR 97448-9559
(541) 998-1873
e-mail: ergo.efn.org • website: www.finalexit.org

ERGO supports choice and, if necessary, help in dying for those who desire it. It advises terminally ill people and their families about euthanasia through literature and online material; its website has extensive resources.

International Anti-Euthanasia Task Force (IAETF)
PO Box 760, Steubenville, OH 43952
(740) 282-3810
e-mail: info@iaetf.org • website: www.iaetf.org

The task force opposes euthanasia, assisted suicide, and policies that threaten the lives of the medically vulnerable. IAETF publishes fact sheets and position papers on euthansia-related topics in addition to the bimonthly newsletter *IAETF Update*. It analyzes the policies and legislation concerning medical and social work organizations and files amicus curiae briefs in major right-to-die cases.

Not Dead Yet
7521 Madison St., Forest Park, IL 60130
(708) 209-1500 • fax: (708) 209-1735
website: www.notdeadyet.org

This national grassroots disability rights organization opposes legalization of physician-assisted suicide and euthanasia because of risks such actions present to disabled and chronically ill people.

Oregon Death with Dignity Legal Defense and Education Center
818 S.W. Third Ave., Suite 218, Portland, OR 97204
(503) 228-6079
e-mail: info@dwd.org • website: www.dwd.org

This group provides information, education, research, and support for a comprehensive range of end-of-life options, including physician-assisted suicide under certain conditions. It works to defend and educate people about Oregon's Death with Dignity Act.

For Further Research

Books

Laura K. Egendorf, ed., *Current Controversies: Assisted Suicide*. San Diego: Greenhaven Press, 1998.

Peter G. Filene, *In the Arms of Others: A Cultural History of the Right-to-Die in America*. Chicago: Ivan R. Dee, 1998.

Derek Humphry and Mary Clement, *Freedom to Die: People, Politics, and the Right-to-Die Movement*. New York: St. Martin's, 1998.

John Keown, ed., *Euthanasia Explained: Ethical, Clinical, and Legal Perspectives*. New York: Cambridge University Press, 1995.

Edward J. Larson and Darrel W. Amundsen, *A Different Death: Euthanasia in the Christian Tradition*. Downers Grove, IL: Intervarsity, 1998.

Charles F. McKhann, *A Time to Die: The Place for Physician Assistance*. New Haven, CT: Yale University Press, 1999.

Jonathan D. Moreno, ed., *Arguing Euthanasia: The Controversy over Mercy Killing*. New York: Simon and Schuster, 1995.

Wesley J. Smith, *Forced Exit: The Slippery Slope from Assisted Suicide to Legalized Murder*. New York: Times Books, 1997.

Michael M. Uhlmann, ed., *Last Rights?: Assisted Suicide and Euthanasia Debated*. Grand Rapids, MI: William B. Eerdmans, 1998.

Sue Woodman, *Last Rights: The Struggle over the Right to Die*. New York: Plenum, 1998.

Lisa Yount, *Euthanasia*. San Diego: Lucent Books, 2001.

Marjorie B. Zucker, *The Right to Die Debate: A Documentary History*. Westport, CT: Greenwood, 1999.

Periodicals

Wybo Algra, "A Release from Life," *UNESCO Courier*, July 2001.

Bruce Barcott, "Dale's Dilemma," *Life*, September 1, 1999.

Daniel Callahan, "Good Strategies and Bad: Opposing Physician-Assisted Suicide," *Commonweal*, December 3, 1999.

Courtney S. Campbell, "Give Me Liberty and Death: Assisted Suicide in Oregon," *Christian Century*, May 5, 1999.

Jonathan Cohn, "Snuff Film," *New Republic*, December 14, 1998.

Ezekiel J. Emanuel, "The End of Euthanasia? Death's Door," *New Republic*, May 17, 1999.

Carol Bernstein Ferry, "A Good Death," *Nation*, September 17, 2001.

Steve Hallock, "Physician-Assisted Suicide: 'Slippery Slope' or Civil Right?" *Humanist*, July/August 1996.

Herbert Hendin, "Physician-Assisted Suicide: A Look at the Netherlands," *Current*, December 1997.

John F. Kavanaugh, "Euthanizing Life," *America*, May 7, 2001.

Jack Kevorkian, "A Modern Inquisition," *Utne Reader*, March/April 1995.

John Leo, "Dancing with Dr. Death," *U.S. News & World Report*, March 22, 1999.

David B. McCurdy, "Saying What We Mean," *Christian Century*, July 17, 1996.

David Miller, "From Life to Death in a Peaceful Instant," *Humanist*, May 2000.

Jeffrey Rosen, "What Right to Die?" *New Republic*, June 24, 1996.

Index

abortion, legalized
  as beginning of a slippery slope, 30
  cartoons on, 31, 33
active euthanasia, 10, 17
  see also physician-assisted suicide
Adkins, Janice, 46
advance directives, 12
American Medical Association (AMA), 38
Anderson, Kirk, 24–25
animals, 24–25, 26–27
Asay, Chuck, 26–27, 55–56
Ashcroft, John, 15, 39

Bacon, Francis, 8
Benson, Steve, 46–47
Bok, Chip, 31–32

Canada, 12–13
cartoonists. *See names of individual cartoonists*
cartoons
  on connection between euthanasia and
    abortion, 31, 33
  criticizing HMOs, 35–36
  criticizing Jack Kevorkian, 46–47,
    48–49
  criticizing medical profession, 20–21
  criticizing U.S. Supreme Court, 57–58
  on euthanasia for pets vs. people,
    24–25, 26–27
  on legislation prohibiting physicians,
    42–43
  mocking anti-euthanasia activists, 53–54
  opposing physician-assisted suicide,
    40–41, 44–45
  on patient's fear of mercy killing, 22
Christianity, 10–11
comatose patients. *See* patients, comatose
Cruzan, Nancy, 12, 53–54
Cruzan v. Director, Missouri Dept. of Health,
  12, 53

Death with Dignity Act (1994), 15

Dority, Barbara, 30

euthanasia
  cartoons on
    legalized abortion and, 31, 33
    for pets vs. people, 24–25, 26–27
  coining of term, 8
  continuing debate on, 17
  controversy over, 8–9
    ancient, 10
    modern, 11
    religious vs. secular, 10–11
  defined, 9
  slippery slope argument on, 29–30
  types of, 9–10
  voluntary, 30
    acceptance of, 12–13
    defined, 9
    Supreme Court's endorsement of, 12
  see also physician-assisted suicide

family members, 9, 11–12
*Final Exit: The Practice of Self-Deliverance
  and Assisted Suicide for the Dying*
  (Humphrey), 13

Gamble, Ed, 33–34
Greeks, 10

Hackler, Chris, 17
health care costs, 16
Hippocrates, 10
Hippocratic oath, 10, 40, 41
HMOs (health maintenance
  organizations), 16, 35–36
Holland, 29–30
hospice care, 14
Humphrey, Derek, 13, 16–17

involuntary euthanasia, 17
  defined, 9
  physician-assisted suicide leading to, 30

Islam, 10–11

Judaism, 10–11

Kamisur, Yale, 15–16
Kevorkian, Jack, 39
    cartoons on, 46–47, 48–49

legislation
    against assisted suicide, lawsuits on, 14,
        51–52
    legalizing physician-assisted suicide,
        14–15, 38–39, 40
    on prohibitions against physicians, 43
living wills, 12
Lynn, Joanne, 16

mercy killing. See euthanasia
Miller, John L., 14

New England Journal of Medicine, 13
New Jersey State Supreme Court, 12

Oregon, 15, 39

palliative care, 13–14
passive euthanasia, 9–10
    acceptance of, 12–13
    Supreme Court's endorsement of, 12
patients
    in cartoons
        asking for euthanasia, 20–21
        not wanting euthanasia, 22
        vs. pets, 24–25, 26–27
    comatose
        in cartoons, 53–54
        conscious vs., 19
        family member decision for, 9
        patient rights and, 12
    rights of, 51
Peck, M. Scott, 14
pets, euthanizing, 24–25, 26–27
Pett, Joel, 57–58
physician-assisted suicide, 10
    cartoons on
        legalization of, 40–41
        U.S. Supreme Court's ruling against,
            55–56, 57–58
    continuing debate on, 17
    defined, 9
    evolving into a "duty to die," 15–16
    as going against medical ethics, 38
    health care costs and, 16–17
    legal challenges to, 14–15

legalizing, 38–39
    vs. palliative care, 13–14
    publicatons on, 13
    slippery slope argument on, 29–30
    see also euthanasia; Kevorkian, Jack
physicians
    in cartoons
        as insensitive to suffering, 20
        as playing God, 44–45
        prohibitions against, 42–43
    palliative care training for, 13–14
    see also physician-assisted suicide
Physicians for Mercy, 44

Quill, Timothy E., 13
Quill v. Vacco, 55
Quinlan, Karen Ann, 11–12

Ramirez, Michael, 40–41
Rehnquist, William, 56, 57
Reinhardt, Stephen, 8–9
Roman Catholic Church, 10
Romans, 10

Scalia, Antonin, 57
60 Minutes (television program), 49
Smith, Mike, 35–36
Smith, Wesley J., 29–30
state laws against assisted suicide, 14, 52
states legalizing physician-assisted suicide,
    15, 38–39, 40
Stayskal, Wayne, 22–23, 44–45

Thomas, Clarence, 57
Thompson, Mike, 48–49
Toles, Tom, 20–21, 53–54

U.S. Supreme Court
    in cartoons, 55–56, 57–58
    endorsement of passive voluntary
        euthanasia, 12
    on patient rights, 51
    response to Nancy Cruzan case, 53–54
    upholding state laws against assisted
        suicide, 14, 52

Voltaire, 10
voluntary euthanasia. See euthanasia,
    voluntary

Washington v. Glucksberg, 55
Wright, Don, 42–43

Youk, Thomas, 48–49